UNDERSTANDING HIM

"For Him, From Her"

Authors:

ANA RITA COMPIO REYES

BIMBY MACBS

ISBN:
Hardbound-978-621-470-452-1
MOBI/KINDLE-978-621-470-453-8
Softbound/Paperback-978-621-470-454-5

Published by:
Poetry Planet Book Publishing House
Rosario, Pozorrubio, Pangasinan, Philippines
Contact Number: 09554960094
Email: maritesritumalta@gmail.com

Dedication

This book is dedicated to all the women in the world to learn how to value themselves. When you are empowered you will learn to understand your husband as a partner and better half in life to have longevity in your relationship.

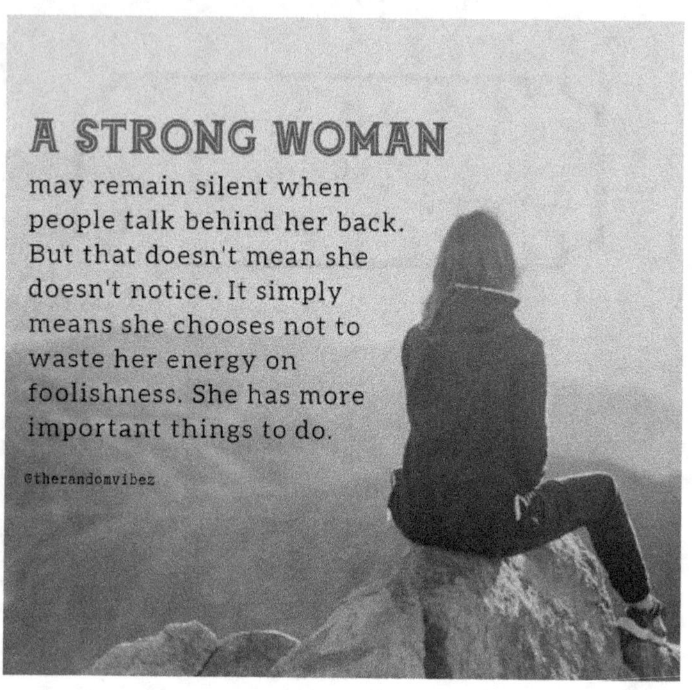

A STRONG WOMAN
may remain silent when
people talk behind her back.
But that doesn't mean she
doesn't notice. It simply
means she chooses not to
waste her energy on
foolishness. She has more
important things to do.

@therandomvibez

Understanding Him
(For Him, From Her)

You don't need to rearrange your life to meet the perfect man. All men are perfect it is only their weaknesses and vague characteristics which brings them to imperfection. And to find a man, it doesn't mean that you have to undergo a series of a transformation of "who you are not" just to satisfy your needs for love and belonging-ness.

This book reveals the thoughts of a man that a woman should need to understand and master to jive with a man's emotions, likes, and interests behaviors which they want to foster in their relationship. This book will help a woman as she enters and prepare for married life or if already married to always fight and sustain love for longevity. To sustain married life and relationship is the true meaning of "Love wins".

Married life is made in heaven but it is not immune from crosses, but if you understand each other and pray for one another, separation will never foster because the grace of God will always keep the love alive.

This book provides 11 rules and guidelines to "Mark" and anticipate in your man to further understand his temperament and thinking.

A woman's mouth should speak of her good heart, her soul should radiate beauty and her strength should offer affection to encourage the man that she loves.

Man will love you unselfishly and will attend to your longings when you know the answer to his questions and needs.

For a woman, beauty is a gift and a good character is a blessing.

For a man, everything that is beautiful in a woman is inscribed in woman's soul.

TABLE OF CONTENTS

With unconditional understanding and companionship, women can create a strong bond with their partner that will last through any challenges they may face in life.

Rule 1: MARK Your Words

If the talk is your passion, make sure it is wise and modest when you are around with your man. Commonly, women are fun of engaging in an argument with an inappropriate response, cursing, swearing and bad jokes if they felt they are losing.

Goofing around can be fun but make sure that when you make a statement it will not demean or belittle your man's ego. Man has an inert sensitivity which can only be manifested when a man will just keep silent when he is offended by your words. He will never let it be shown but you can sense it by his gesture and through his simple but deadly remarks.

Criticizing while your boyfriend or spouse is with his pack of friends is impious especially when you are cursing him. Give him consideration and hold your tongue thrice as needed. When you embarrass your man in front of his company his worth will be devalued and his friends will show disrespectful behavior towards him sooner or later as a result of your imprudence.

Do not rumor your boyfriend or broadcast your fight and misunderstanding among your relatives and friends. Whatever you had in your relationship whether it is winning or crying it should be kept between the two of you. No drama on social media! Unless grave verbal and physical abuse is imminent. When you share small issues in your family and friends, when you and your partner reconciled, your significant other's still can't forget and forgive.

Never criticize your boyfriend or spouse's mother. There are qualities in his mother that he found and you so you should be careful in giving your opinion when he verbalizes his feeling if he has a misunderstanding with his mother.

Learn to control your emotions when you are in anger despite of your disappointment with your man. Do not transform your anger into unkind words that will leave a deep wound on his pride. When you keep on repeating his negativity the possible result is that he will accept that negativism and will continue to do that as a never-ending cycle.

Man is like a sponge they will absorb whatever words you feed them. If you will give them sweet, sincere and thoughtful words you can squeeze out gentle and tender words from their inner being.

Sweet words must always come from a woman's lips whether it is better or bitter days, it is expected from you to give a positive reinforcement for your man.

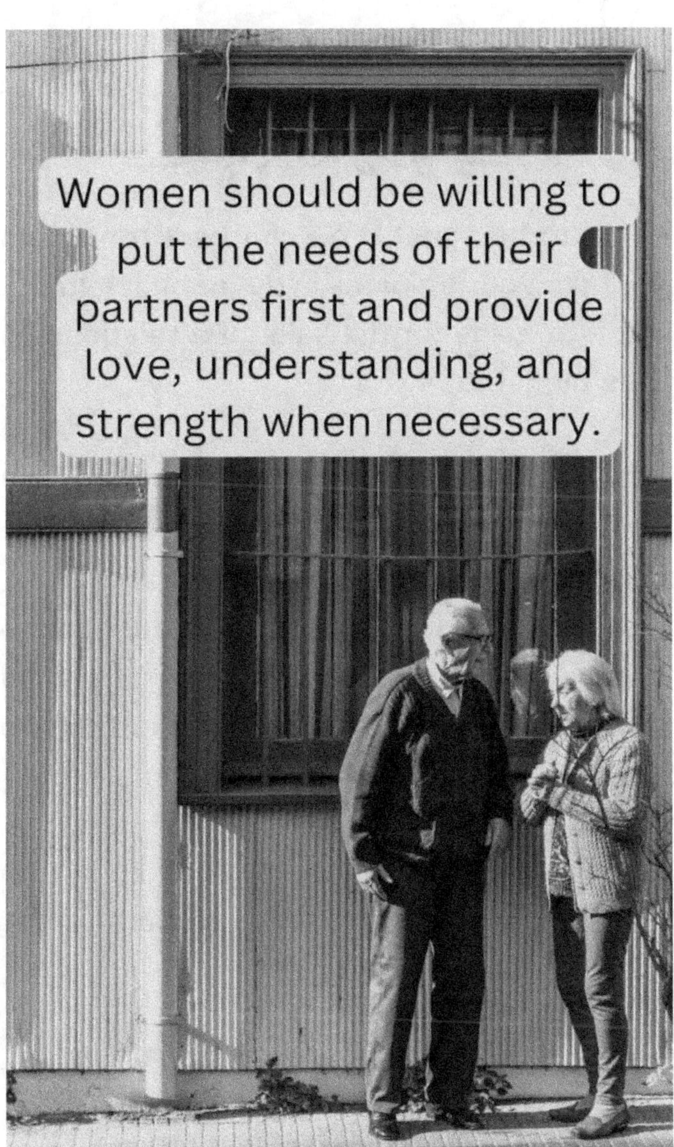

Women should be willing to put the needs of their partners first and provide love, understanding, and strength when necessary.

"You can be smart. You can be strong. You can have your opinions. You just have to put your ego aside for the sake of a relationship that's bigger than you"

Thoughtfulness is one of the basic attractions that a man is looking for in a woman. During the course of courtship, the man always shows an extra effort by giving you flowers and boxes of chocolate not just to please you and to get a good score but this is a reflection of being a man who can provide both temporal and emotional needs.

This is a strong and complete gesture of a man who is being a responsible and efficient partner to be.

Women are ought to be thoughtful too. They must be a giver of hope, motivation, and inspiration for the man they love.

Affection and love are best expressed in thoughtful words plus action. A small note with the words "I miss you even though we are always together" inside a man's pocket will surprise him with your charming gesture of thoughtfulness. It will surely tickle his heart.

Being thoughtful is a sexy attribute next to being smart and honest. It builds a good emotional bond and it offers a place where you can deliberately excite your partner for more fun and exciting relationship.

Try to cook for him for an unknown purpose. Be original and never follow the trend.

If your boyfriend can make huge things for you, do your share by magnifying it too.

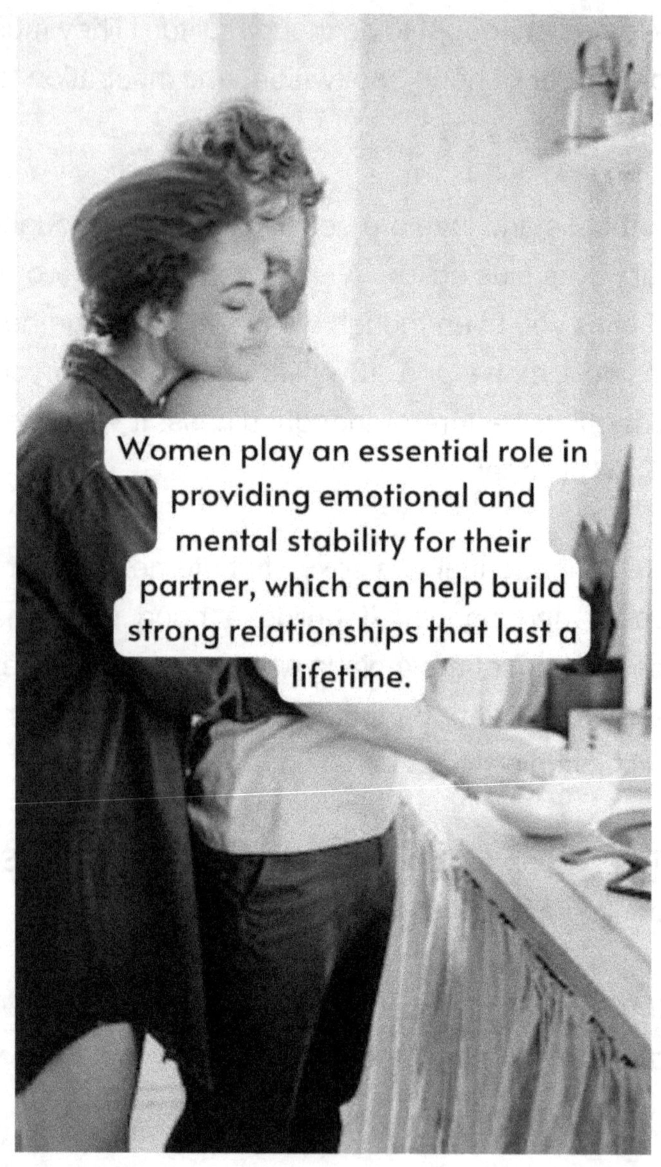

Women play an essential role in providing emotional and mental stability for their partner, which can help build strong relationships that last a lifetime.

Do pretend nothing is wrong with a peal of forced laughter. You wear a smile but you fake your joy.

A woman would always tell their friends that the reason why she broke up with her boyfriend is simply because of a petty misunderstanding. How can you be understood if you can't be brutally honest with what you feel?

Most women avoid confrontation with their partners because of the fear of rejection. But they never realized that there is more than fear if that evasion will lead to separation.

Saying okay when you are not and ignoring pain when you are hurt is a mechanism of the strong but a failure to the brave.

If you feel you are cheated, betrayed, and jealous, tell it right away to your boyfriend or husband. Do not let your partner do the guessing game. If you are fun of riddles then you should have a clairvoyant for a boyfriend.

You can hide several emotions in your eyes but always remember that your tears are real when you are hurt.

Men don't like to feel guilty about your pain without knowing the fact and the real story behind your rumpus and uproar. They want you to vent your real feelings so that they could adjust to your emotional needs.

Men have enough willingness to change for the person they love if they are given pure reason to change. You just need to reassure them of what you want from them and what you expect in a relationship.

A good woman should have a gentle and understanding heart, and a supportive soul that can help her man or husband get through any hard times they may face.

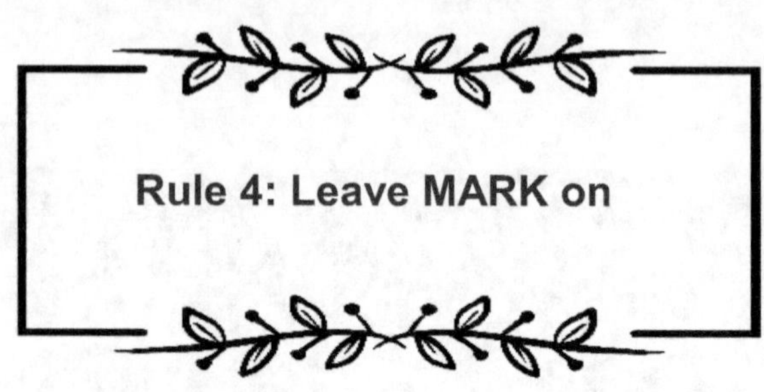

You can't change him. I know that you know it intellectually, but if you think you can pull it off. You can't. And if you manage to get it done, he will figure it out and resent you for it. Love him the way he is not or not at all.

Women usually wanted to twist their men for their own benefit. A woman likes to give their opinion on a man's fashion, interests, sports, and TV shows that he likes without consulting the guy if it is okay for him or not.

"She told me what to do but she never ask my feelings and opinion about it" is a common line that we usually hear from our male friends who are ventilating their emotions about their relationship with their girlfriend. Man doesn't want a bossy and pushy girlfriend.

Whether you are one as a couple, your partner's identity should remain with him. Allow him to be authentic with himself. If his parents can't intervene in his personality then why do you need to impost something?

The merit of love is freedom thus it is necessary to give your boyfriend or spouse his own identity. He will feel secure and loved if you give him his own space to be real and productive of his own accord.

Men are emotionally weak, women are strong in suffering. Support your man all the time.

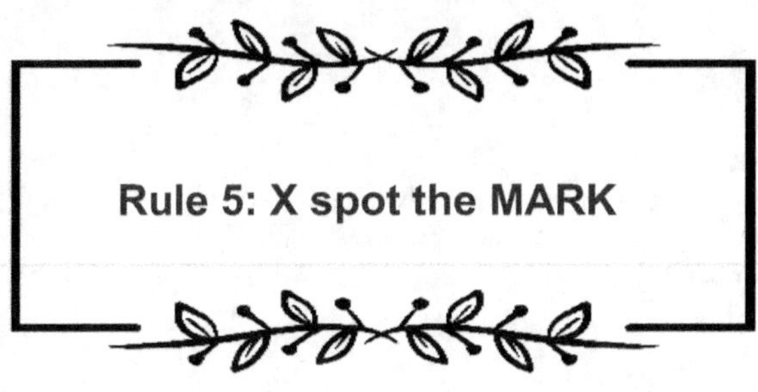

Rule 5: X spot the MARK

Do not ask your husband or partner a question that you are not mature enough to hear and response to.

Hey, he got a bunch of histories in the past so do you. If you allow the previous events from his old self to maim your present relationship you are building a scenario of the nightmare that can't be extinguished by a certain act of contrition.

If you truly love him for being what he is right now, you should never get worried about the steps he took to get there. Your love must overpower all the insecurities and his history must never cripple your present relationship when those memories are no longer existing.

Throwing old arguments and issues from his past will just create more tension, will harbor a loss of trust, and will ultimately change how he looks and feel about you.

If you keep on using his previous commitment to your current situation during your fight your relationship will have a hard time recovering. It could certainly lead to the demise of a relationship.

It is always a poor strategy for a woman to point out prior mistakes in every fight because it will never dignify you but rather will terrify you with its outcome.

Man will always wear his scar but does not return the pain that he has almost forgotten.

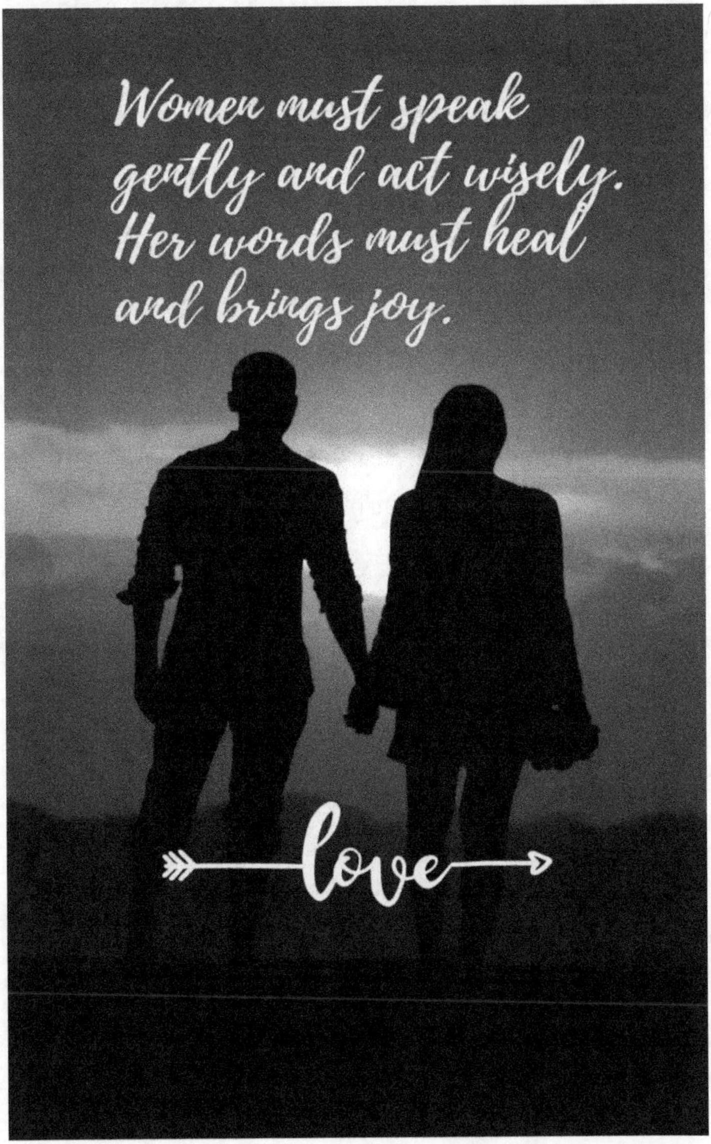

Women must speak
gently and act wisely.
Her words must heal
and brings joy.

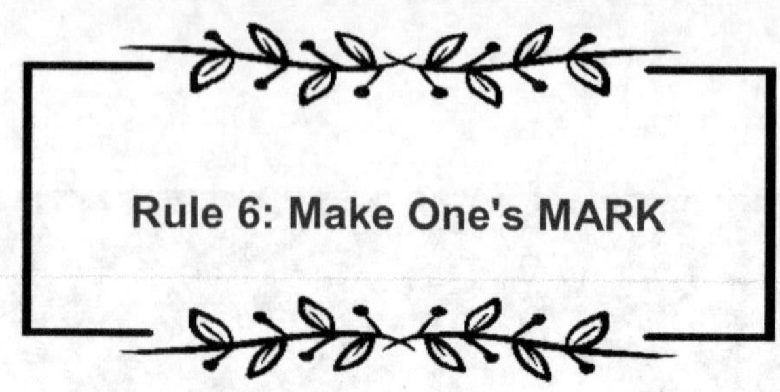

Your man will inevitably get jealous of your friends, especially your straight male friends. If cats and dogs are territorial it is tantamount to your boyfriend or your husband.

Do not try to confide your issues with your man to your male college best friend. Your man will feel and think that you are more at ease in venting your issues to a male friend than resolving them together as a couple.

We understood that our best friend can provide us comfort and shelter in the moment of our heartaches. But sometimes it will cause fire instead of resolution of the issues more specifically when you are in a compromising situation.

What if your male close friend will compare his characteristics to your boyfriend or will dictate and suggest what to do? There are instances that your male friend will also impost on you what you deserve from your man. This will further put more clouds on your thoughts that will disallow you to think wisely and clearly.

If possible, you have to limit meeting your male friends which will cause doubt and tension. We can't avoid circumstances in that, you have to re-kindle friendship because you knew your friend first before your boyfriend and husband however, you have to make sure that you are in a comfort-able and winning situation for both of your male friends and your man.

Another point that you must avoid is flirting with your male friends or give your man an idea that you are fascinated with male friends even if you don't have such intention. Don't risk ruining your friendship and relationship or there will be bad days ahead.

Your man wanted that he is the only guy next to your Dad in your life, so, you must live by it. So, everything in relationship is all about trust, respect, and putting your husband first.

A devoted wife is the secret of a successful marriage.

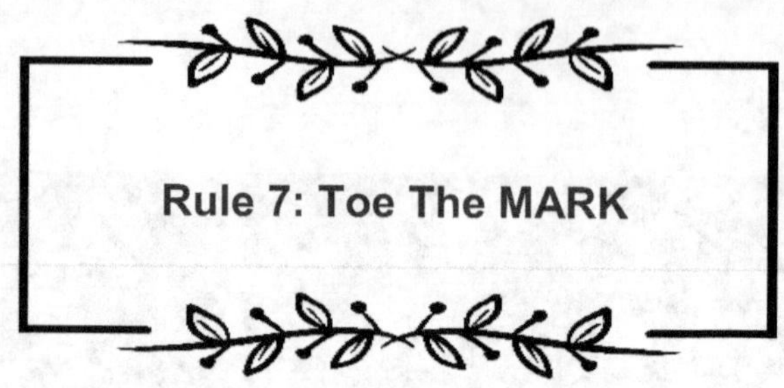

Rule 7: Toe The MARK

"I don't mean to be needy, but I need you to need me."

Man wants that you need him too. Surely, being independent is something that a man is looking for in his woman but there are instances that man wanted to feel his worth and existence through your way of showing how much you need him in your life.

Let him open a bottle of soda for you, cook your favorite dinner, and even up to fetch you from work every day or randomly.

These little gestures will intensify the growth of your relationship because you allow your man to take light responsibility that will suffice his affection to you.

If your boyfriend or husband asks you to give him a chance to do you a favor so be it. It will make him feel useful and it will boost his self-esteem.

Give your man a challenge to give you a fish and he will truly give you the entire school of fish.

The partnership of man and woman is a shared relationship. Sometimes you must allow your man to do his way of expressing his love to you to further nurture the affair.

But wait, He is not your Father. Do not look for the quality of your father to your husband or partner now. Transforming him to be someone he is not will just create disorder.

For all you princesses out there. Yes, he's supposed to take care of you, but it's not in the same way as your father did. You're a grown woman, for Heaven's sake, learn the difference between the care of a father and the love of your partner and do not get confuse of it.

A woman is truly a gem for her husband when she puts in the effort to make sure that everyone in the family is well taken care of.

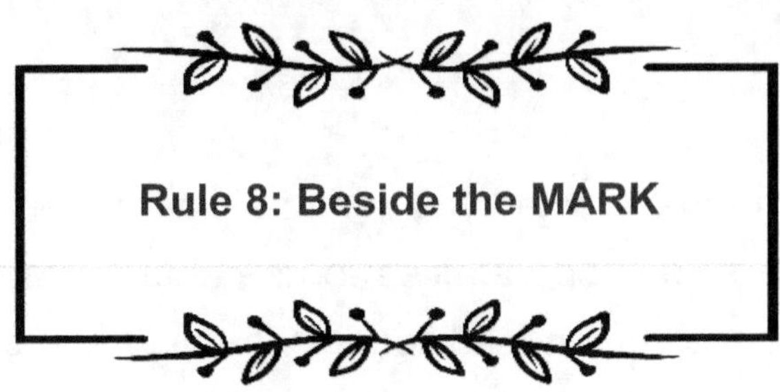

Rule 8: Beside the MARK

He wants you to be on his side.

Behind every great man is an excellent woman. Your man needs someone who will be there for him, who will listen to his hopes and dreams. Every man on the planet is searching and praying for a woman who will inspire him to keep going.

If you abandon him at parties and go talk to your friends while he talks to his, you're not giving him that level of completion he wants in a partner. Sure, you can branch out now and then, but he wants you to work as a duo.

Your man needs you too as much as you need him. You are not just his partner but you are a co-creator of his aspiration in life. He needs your sweet attention.

Your man expected you to make big troubles turn into a small opportunities to rise again with your presence and unconditional love. Always support your man as long it is morally right and under the context of your sincere obedience. Men are always weak thus, you must support them all the time. Women are strong in circumstances and sufferings. Your inner strength will propel and empower your husband.

By the end being devoted and
obedient, a woman has the
capability to create harmony
between herself, her husband, their
children, and any other members of
their extended family.

Rule 9: MARKS On Your Knee

Prayer plays a big role in relationships. It is a must that your relationship is always inclined to God's will. The husband is the leader of the home and his leadership can save the whole family while the woman represents the mercy and grace of God.

A wise woman is a gift to a man but a Godly woman is a blessing to a man, her family unto their future generations. A woman should always stand as the moral compass for her man.

A woman should be the channel of love, hope, and faith in a relationship. She will encompass the grace of God through her devotion that will efficiently radiate into the heart of his partner to be faithful to God too.

Man will never go wrong with a woman who has Christian values. She will bring honor and a good name for his partner. She will be a gem that will shines brightly.

Please remember, we are not out on a hunting party trying to find meat for supper, but we are in pursuit of a life partner who we can love, cherish, and lead. Relationship as exciting as it is also a huge responsibility.

In your affair, your question will always be "Do I want my boyfriend or husband to be in a relationship with God?", "While my boyfriend or husband will represent the leadership of God in our family life?"

Through respect for each other's wishes and understanding of one another's limitations, a woman can become an invaluable asset in any household.

Be quick in complimenting your boyfriend or your partner. Telling your man how he plays well in soccer or how his new pair of sneakers complement him is gratifying to your boyfriend's ego. He will feel secure and confident. Do not delay gratification.

Always give the best part of the chicken to him. He deserves not just the first best but also the second until the third best as a way of thanking him for all his effort of loving you from the day of courting until you are in a relationship together.

For young ladies, your virginity is only for your husband, if you give it to another man, then you stole it from your future husband. However, you may restore your lost grace by asking God's forgiveness through repentance and live in spiritual virginity through chastity until you get married in the church. That is the best gift you can give to him.

Always encourage your husband and reinforce your love and care for him day by day. Send him some random messages during his busy day that will inspire him and will lighten him with what he is doing at that moment.

Teach him some simple skills like baking or doing some cross-stitching and gardening. It will be a good nurturing moment for the two of you. It will improve your bond and will develop a sense of attachment and closeness.

He wants you to like what he is fascinated about. Whether it is in sports, fitness, and hobbies. Even if it is not a cup of your tea but merely loving things that he usually fond of will make him feel important and interesting.

He wants that you bring something special and extra into his life.

Be a woman that he will be proud of. A woman who is smart and always at her best in her looks and appearance every time you are together.

A woman's simplicity brings joy to man and it is a treasure that brings a lasting relationship

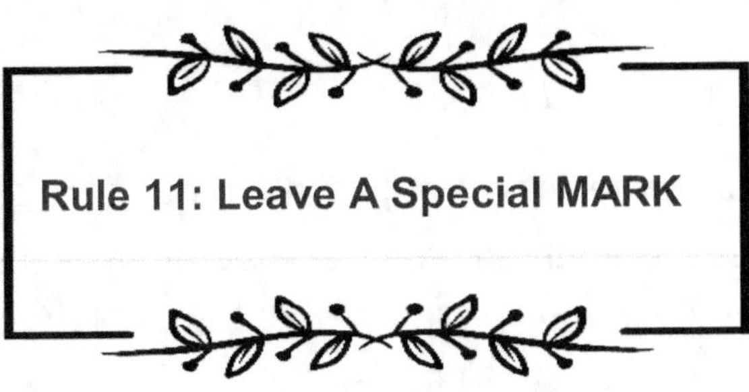

Rule 11: Leave A Special MARK

Whether the relationship will progress or will get done instantly due to several concerns make sure that you leave him with wonderful memories and amazing stories about you that will linger in his heart for a lifetime.

Even the best relationship will fall down some-times regardless of how you are devoted to each other. It is not always guaranteed that love will preserve your relationship. It will always include sacrifices and a series of constant encouraging communication.

Man is always the provider of physical, spiritual, and emotional needs but the woman should be the Paraclete or the advocate of what the man will provide. As a woman, you should invest in nurtur-ing your man through your wholesome discipline and inner goodness.

Be a partner and not just a girlfriend. A partner will see everything beyond what the eyes can see while a girlfriend will just enjoy the whole game that was presented to her.

Your essence as a woman is to become a mystery to your man and part of that mystery is being a woman full of interesting surprises and a woman with an untainted character.

Men will crave a woman
with a beautiful
soul.

Final MARKing

Being perfect isn't easy, but it's totally achievable if you know what your guy really wants. Guys have different perceptions of what they consider a "perfect girlfriend" to be, but still, the stuff most of us agree are good qualities in a girlfriend. Women are not the only ones looking for their soul mate, "the One" is a guy's goal too.

- YouQueen.Com

A woman should know these three important in-gredients to win the heart of a man.

The knowledge to feel and understand the drives and needs of his man. The skills that she needs to master to be appealing to his man (including the skill of making beautiful and pleasing all the time) and above all the attitude that will drive him knocks off of his feet.

Build your own Cinderella Story and make it real. Nurture it with prayer, courage and joy.

Marriage life and relationship is always for the strong, because every day you need to forgive.

ABOUT THE AUTHORS

Ana Rita Reyes is an educator, ECE Program Director, Admin, and Co-Creator of FIL-AM SOUTH BAY COMMUNITY, Commissioner of Library and Education in District 5 San Jose, California, Motivational Speaker, Transformational Life Coach, and a Catechist.

She is been the author of 3 books. Her autobiography "Woman Of Hope" and self-help books "365 Days" and "I am Worthy" co-authored 2 self-help guide books for a couple "Understanding Him" and "Understanding Her".

She is also a writer and co-author of 3 Children's book which showcases Philippine Culture, and Stories about values and teachers.

She is featured on the cover of Planet Magazines where her stories and works were depicted.

She has been featured on TV for her altruistic work in the community, interviewed on Radio and podcasts, and received various awards and recognition for her unparalleled service to the community. Interviewed with local, national, and international media outlets like Canada, the USA, and the Philippines.

Internationally earned a Doctorate in Literature through her 1st book Woman of Hope

Her life is dedicated to being a service to the community through service, altruism, and promoting physical, emotional, intellectual, and spiritual change through her blogs and writings on social media and daily Facebook Live inspirational talk and guest speaker for school.

She has a little foundation with a friend called "Woman Of Hope Foundation" by the annual Christmas "Adopt A Kid" and they are supporting selected kids in their schooling.

Her passion and dedication to her career and personal endeavors are driven by love and selflessness for the greater glory of God.

Bimby Macbs is a Registered Nurse in the Philippines and has worked in Academe and Pharmaceutical Companies.

He decides to discontinue his job and focus on freelance writing, catechism, and in evangelization.

He has training in the human temperament, love languages, and psycho-spiritual integration.

He is a career coach (helping students in matching their character to their career toward a successful college program and professional life) lyricist, poet, writer, event host, organizer, administrator of local celebrities' online platform, and author of a published children's book.

"When You Really Love Someone"
~Alicia Keys

I'm a woman
Lord knows it's hard
I need a real man
To give me what I need
Sweet attention
Love and tenderness
When it's real, it's unconditional
I'm telling y'all

'Cause a man just ain't a man if he ain't man enough
To love you when you're right
Love you when you're wrong
Love you when you're weak
Love you when you're strong
Take you higher
When the world's got you feeling low
He's giving you his last
'Cause he's thinking of you first
Giving comfort when he's thinking that you're hurt
That's what done when you really love someone
I'm telling y'all, I'm telling y'all

'Cause you're a real man
And lord knows it's hard
Sometimes you just need a woman's touch
Sweet affection
Love and support
When it's real, it's unconditional
I'm telling y'all

Oh, 'cause a woman ain't a woman if she ain't
woman enough
To love you when you're right
Love you when You're wrong
Love you when you're weak
Love you when you're strong
Take you higher, oh
When the world's got you feeling low
She giving you her best
Even when you're at your worst
Giving 'comfort when she's thinking that you're hurt
That's what's done when you really love someone
I'm telling y'all, I'm telling y'all

Sometimes you wanna argue, sometimes you wanna fight
Sometimes it's gonna feel like it'll never be right
But something so strong keeps you holding on
It's don't make sense, but it makes a good song

'Cause a man just ain't a man if he ain't man enough
To love you when you're right
Love you when you're wrong
Love you when you're weak
Love you when you're strong
Take you higher
When the world's got you feeling low
He's giving you his last
'Cause he's thinking of you first
Giving comfort when he's thinking that you're hurt
That's what's done when you really love someone
I'm telling y'all, I'm telling y'all

I'm telling y'all that a woman ain't a woman
If she ain't woman enough
To love you when you're right
Love you when you're wrong
Love you when you're weak
Love you when you're strong
Take you higher (And higher)
When the world's got you feeling low
She giving you her best
Even when you're at your worst
Giving comfort when she's thinking that you're hurt
That's what's done when you really love someone
I'm telling y'all, I'm telling y'all

www.ingramcontent.com/pod-product-compliance
Lightning Source LLC
LaVergne TN
LVHW021007200726
843506LV00012B/2218